SIMPLE HACKS THAT CAN HELP AN AGING OR ACHING BODY

Simple Hacks That Can Help an Aging or Aching Body

Simple Positions or Tricks to Help Ease Aches and Pains

EMY LOU DANA

BareTreeCrafts21

Contents

This is dedicated to my family, my dad Marcelo, my mom, Noemi, and my two brothers Lito and Nonoy who have already joined our parents in heaven. To my only sibling left, my sister, who helped me to be where I am today. To my nephews and nieces. To my beloved husband, Paul.

Chapter 1

Introduction

Hello, my name is Emy Lou Dana, and I have worked as a physical therapist for about 20 years. I worked with the elderly and young adults in different settings, such as long-term care facilities, outpatient clinics, and home care, the last at a hospital or acute care setting. As a person suffering from migraines for a long time since I was in college, I learned to understand my body. I knew my body was not as strong as it should be compared to regular healthy women who do not suffer from ailments such as migraines. Now and then, I hurt my muscles or joints, such as my wrists, from everyday chores at home. So I learned these little tricks to help ease the pain or help prevent further damage to my wrist or any part of my body.

I wanted to write this book in a way that is easy to understand and that people will benefit from it. These little hacks or tips are so simple that anyone can do it and temporarily relieve their aches or pains to feel comfortable when sleeping at night. I used these tricks whenever I needed them and made a difference.

If for some reason, you are uncomfortable, or if the pain worsens, you can always ask your doctor or physical therapist or stop and don't do the position or exercise. Use your judgment when the pain gets worse or more severe. Then, most likely, that is not the right position for you. Remember that I do not intend to replace any medical advice from your doctor or physical therapist if you see one now. Also, I want to emphasize doing these positions or exercises slowly and gently as it is intended to ease the ache or pain and not make it worse. I will not be responsible if you hurt yourself. Always use caution while trying to position yourself.

You can follow me on social media or connect with my posts on Facebook, Instagram, or Pinterest (Emy Dana or BareTreeCrafts21).

Chapter 2

The Wrist Hack

Have you ever felt that your wrist does not feel right at times? It is incredibly annoying when you are trying to sleep at night, and it feels like your wrist can't seem to relax, or you can't get comfortable enough. You are wondering what you did or did to your wrist. You might have twisted or overstretched it while washing the dishes or doing yard work. Well, one thing I found very helpful is keeping a small washcloth or a sock in your hand as if you are holding a small ball or washcloth while you sleep at night. Or you can use a small pillow to prop your hand so it's in a resting position. I will tell you about the resting position in a bit.

Or, if you don't like to use a washcloth or don't like to hold something in your hand, or maybe you lost it in the middle of the night, you can try laying on one side and using a small pillow or regular pillow or a towel to position your wrist comfortably. The goal is to extend the wrist slightly with fingers flexed or curled. Yes, this is the resting position. If you have injured your wrist or hand badly, maybe fractured, or had tendonitis, you are probably familiar with wearing a wrist splint or a wrist brace. This gives support and immobilizes the joint for a short time to prevent it from re-injuring that joint again, so it can properly heal. Or maybe you have carpal tunnel; the splint is advised to wear as a conservative or first step to manage the pain. Using a wrist brace will benefit you depending on how severe your discomfort is. You may have to do this trick for a day or two to a few days or longer if needed. It is best to watch out for common position or movement that aggravates the pain or discomfort. One thing, especially for women who washes dishes with their hands, it is best to rest or put the plate down on the side of the countertop, on top of a washcloth or dishrag (to give a cushion or protection between the dish and the countertop), so you take some of the weight of the dish and not strain your wrist. In other words, you are getting help by not holding the dish with one hand while the other hand is scrubbing the dish. This way, you have the leverage when holding, especially when you have a heavy plate. You are mainly preventing your wrist from overstraining and overuse injuries.

I would say that repetitive or overuse wrist injuries are prevalent as we always tend to do everything with our hands. That means the pain will tell you that something is inflamed and not right and that it needs to rest for that part to heal. It is always best to slow down, be aware of how we move our hand or wrist, and try to prevent those movements that aggravate it for a little while. One example is that I washed the floor mop with my hands one day after mopping the floor. The following day, I got this pain in my right thumb while doing the dishes and noticed that my thumb was a bit swollen or inflamed. So what I did was I just tried to avoid the movement that aggravated it while trying to use or hold on to the small washcloth when sleeping at night to keep it in a comfortable position. I tried to use more of my left hand and switched or changed the way I did things that day. I tried to rest my wrist or hand, especially my thumb. And the next day, I didn't feel any pain at all. I just tried to be careful by being aware of how I move my wrist while doing my chores. I usually do this until I don't feel that pain anymore. This is what I learned about my body. I would get a little discomfort or ache after certain new activities or movements that my body was not used to. I knew it was nothing severe, and I didn't need anti-inflammatory medicine, especially when the pain only comes with specific movements or is not too bad when resting. And it will just go away if I give it time to heal and rest.

Here is a picture of that resting position for the hand and wrist. And I would use the same trick or work for the thumb, just like the wrist. Using the washcloth trick or a small ball (even a sock) on your hand when you sleep at night will also help keep the thumb in the right or resting position. You will feel the difference when trying to sleep because as

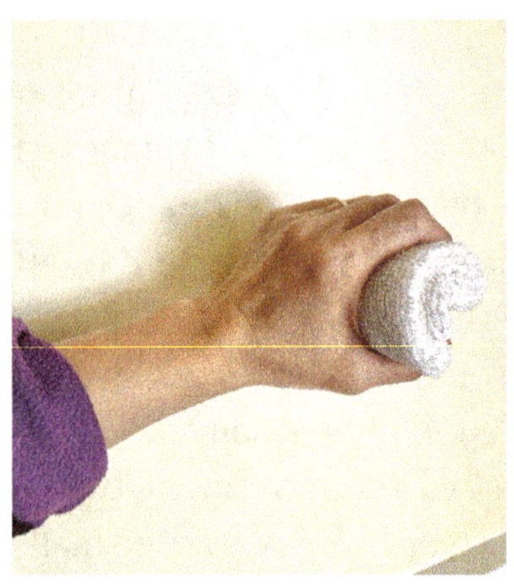

Wrist in a slightly extended position and fingers flexed or half closed.

soon as you put that hand or wrist in the resting position, you can feel that your wrist is more relaxed and less painful or achy. I usually have a small soft towel (or washcloth) on my bed, and whenever I feel like I need to use it, I try to hold it in whatever position I am in my sleep at night. The main thing is that you keep that towel or washcloth so your wrist or hand is in a resting position. You have to find the correct position with it that you find most comfortable.

Front view of the wrist in resting
position.

Another tip or hack for the wrist of thumb is that when you are trying to get on your hands and knees on the floor or just try-ing to crawl on the bed, it is always best when you keep your wrist or hand closed, like making a fist and putting your weight on your knuckles or the fist. This position is the closed-pack position of the fingers

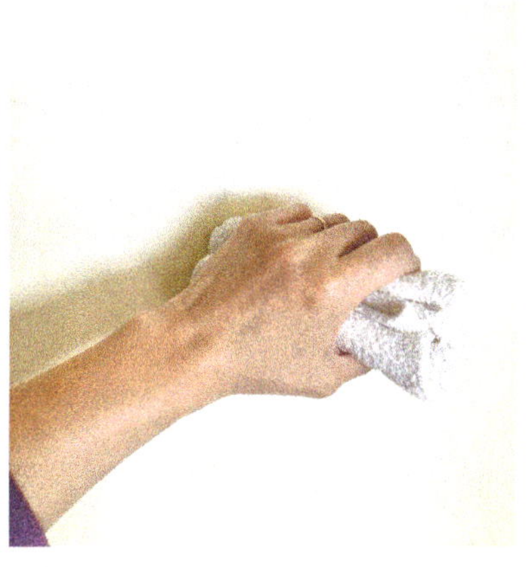

Wrist in resting position, with wrist more in a neutral position (neither extended nor flexed).

and wrist joints, making it more stable and less likely to

overstretch any ligaments or tendons in your wrist, thus causing less or no pain.

Another thing I usually do when my wrist doesn't feel right or just a little uncomfortable I would do this trick or movement. It's a stretching exercise for the wrist; you can do this with both hands, bringing them close to you or your chest, then slowly and gently moving them in front of you like pushing something forwards. Hold it in that position for a few seconds and repeat it a few times. Of course, this might not be the proper exercise for you if you feel severe pain.

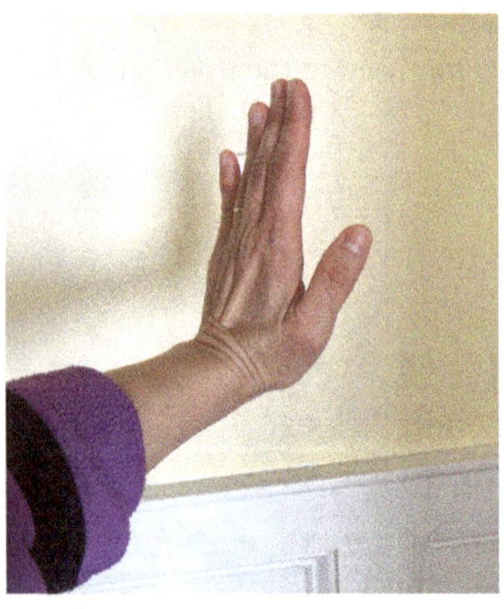

Like pushing your hands in front of you.

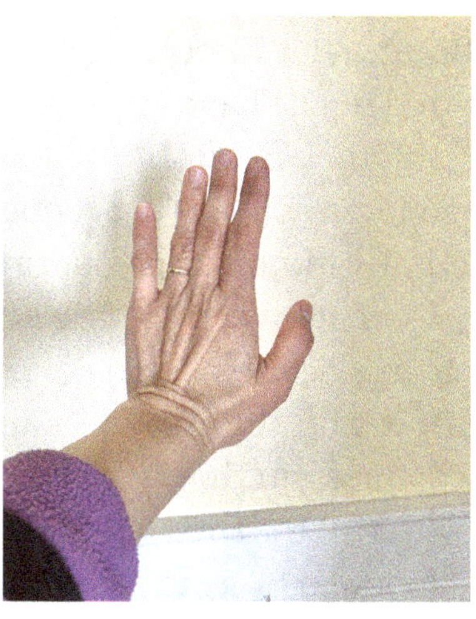

The back of the hand or wrist with
tendons markedly showing.

In addition to the wrist, another thing about the hand or wrist is the finger, one thing common, I would say, is the trigger finger. If you are unfamiliar with it, it is a condition when the finger's tendon sheath becomes irritated and swollen, making it harder for the tendon to glide through the sheath that, causes the finger to get locked in a flexed position or finger to be unable to straighten or extend. This is primarily a repetitive injury to the finger and people constantly using their hands, such as repetitive gripping (for example, opening soda pop cans or doing crafts). People with medical conditions such as diabetes, osteoarthritis, rheumatoid arthritis, or gout are predisposed to this problem. If you think you are just getting a trigger finger, the best advice I can give you is to avoid the movement that causes it. I know it is impossible if you have a job where you have to use your hands or fingers. But if you can, avoid or switch the hand every so often so one hand can rest and avoid over-using it. Then, a warm compress on the affected finger even about 10 minutes, followed by gentle stretching of the finger. And lastly, try to keep your fingers in a resting position by holding a washcloth when sleeping or whenever you are resting. Same thing to the wrist; if you feel a slight stiffness on the back of your wrist, a nice warm(not hot) compress on the back of the wrist (as you can see in the picture of the wrist, you have tendons that cross the wrist), followed by gentle stretching by moving it up and down or moving small circles with it. And, of course, keeping it in a resting position when sleeping or resting. Sometimes, people need trigger finger surgery as the condition gets worse. The key is to take care of the affected finger at the first sign or symptom.

Overall, the wrist or hand can be a little tricky because it is hard not to use it, but if you can give it time to rest for a couple of days or a few days, you can make your hand or wrist feel better. In the meantime, try to use the other hand more to give the affected hand a break or time to rest and heal.

Chapter 3

Neck Hack

Have you ever felt uncomfortable on your neck while trying to sleep at night? Maybe you were working in front of the computer or desk for a long time, or you must have turned your neck the wrong way. One tip is to check your pillow and ensure you have enough support on the back of your neck. Our neck has a little curve called lordosis, your standard anatomical curve. This part needs good support when you lay flat or sideways. So you want to ensure you have a nice firm pillow to help support this part of your neck.

I would invest in a good, firm pillow. A soft, fluffy, or thin pillow will not help an aching neck. If you're a very lightweight or skinny person, it might do it, but the main thing is that you get good support on this so-called curve on the back of your neck. Just like the wrist, you want to maintain that resting position on your neck, which is a neutral position, and a nice firm pillow does that. You want to keep the neck in a neutral position. The neck should be either flexed or bent or extended. A slightly extended neck is the best position when sleeping. If you don't have a firm pillow, try a small roll or hand towel and put it behind your neck while lying on your back. You can also place that towel between your cheek and chin (or under your jaw near your ear) to keep your head or neck from bending too much on the side, which can cause a stiff neck.

Another benefit of this firm pillow which keeps your neck's natural or resting position, is that it maintains your airway so you can get enough air in and out of your lungs. In other words, it helps to keep you from snoring as well. And you can rest well when you get up in the morning. I would say this neck pain is probably prevalent nowadays, especially for those who work long hours in front of the computer. Neck muscles get strained or overused this way, leaning over your computer or hunching over. Another common cause of neck pain is just plain aging or osteoarthritis of the neck or spine. One thing to know is when you have numbness or loss of strength in your arms or hand, or maybe a shooting pain in your shoulder or down your arm, then that is the time you will need to consult your doctor as soon as you can.

And yes, if you have severe pain from an injury such as a motor vehicle accident or fall, you will need immediate care. Also, if you have severe pain that persists for days without relief or if it spreads down your arm and has numbness or headache. Then, you will also need to see a doctor. As part of trying to get relief by adequately positioning your neck during sleep, I would like to impart that it is best to prevent neck pain by being aware of your posture. Yes, you want to avoid forward head posture. That is when your neck slants forward, placing your head in front of your shoulders. It increases stress on your spine and leads to muscle strain or tightness of neck muscles. Another way to prevent it is by doing stretching exercises for your neck. Just move the neck forwards, backward, and sidewards gently. Yes, you are just moving it to the normal motions of the neck, pain-free movements. And the main thing is doing it gently, just to the limit of the range of motion of your neck. You don't want to force it, and you want to stop it if you get sharp or intense pain. Here are some pictures of proper neck positioning: My picture shows the appropriate neck position when sleeping on your back.

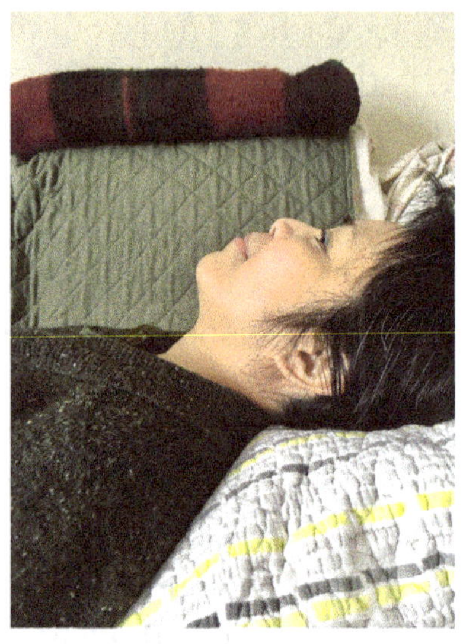

It might not be the best picture to demonstrate the correct neck position, but you get the idea that the neck should be supported well by the pillow. An excellent firm pillow, so it gives the back of your neck where that curve is and gets good support. The head is slightly extended and not bent forwards. At least, I find that works better for me, as it keeps the airway open. Another tip is to roll a small towel and put it on the side of my jaw or the neck on one side, as shown in the picture below. This way, it supports the jaw and keeps the neck from too much bending to the side or lateral flexion. With the jaw supported also, it keeps the tongue in place and helps from snoring. Snoring indicates the air is not correctly coming in or out freely in your nose, throat, and lungs. The towel also keeps you from getting a stiff neck from too much bending to the side. I also use any soft cloth like a little throw blanket or a soft t-shirt, and I roll it nicely or just put it in whatever way I can as long as I get the right support. Once you get that feeling of proper or resting position when resting on your neck, you will know how to position that pillow or the towel for support. And, of course, as you change your position on the bed, you may want to do it slowly and gently so as not to hurt or strain your neck or other muscles.

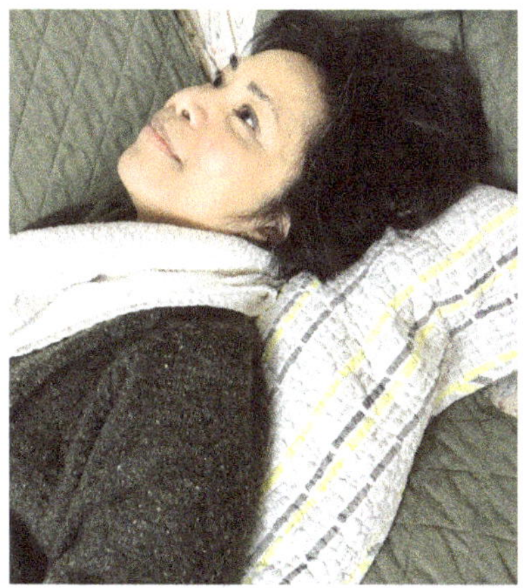

I use a towel to support the head,
keep it from rolling to the side and
support the neck or jaw.

Chapter 4

The Shoulder Hack

Have you ever felt some discomfort in your shoulder? You know it's alright, but it has that discomfort or slight pain when you try to move a certain way. Well, whatever you did, maybe you tried playing a little tennis for the first time, or you did something that you are not used to doing, perhaps you did a little too much of a specific activity, putting a strain on your shoulder, or maybe you just basically tried to reach for something or tried to reach back to scratch your back. Well, the best tip I can give is when lying down on your back, you can use a pillow or a rolled towel on your side to rest that arm on the pillow by the elbow and up to the shoulder. Put it so your arm is level or parallel with the bed.

You will feel relief and know that the arm or shoulder is fully supported and that muscles can relax. Sometimes, I would do both sides of my shoulders as I felt comfortable.

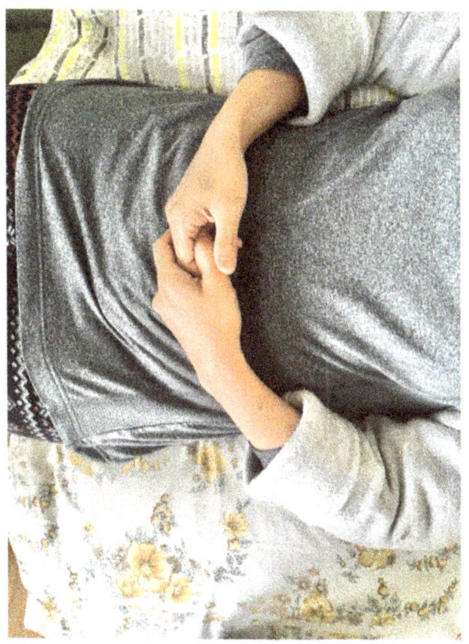

Top view, both elbows are
supported by pillows on each side.

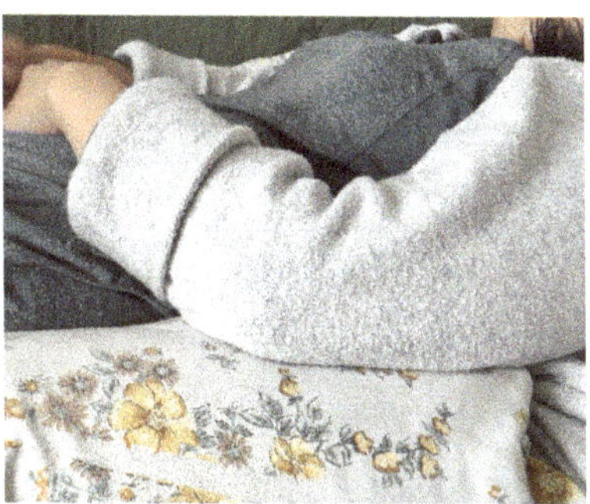

Side view

Another position is lying on your back; you put a pillow to prop your arm on your side, as shown here:

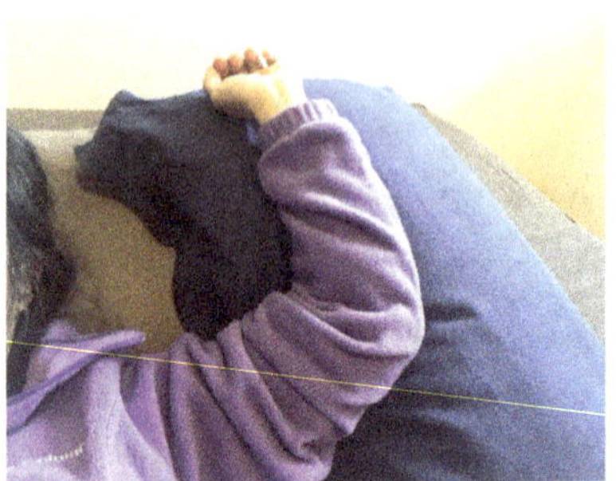

Top view with the arm supported
by a pillow.

You can reposition or adjust the pillow in a way that is more comfortable for you. Another position is when you want to lay on your side and have a pillow between your arms as if you are hugging the pillow. This will keep your arms or shoulders in a neutral or resting position.

Another tip when your shoulder doesn't feel right or uncomfortable during the day is to rest or put your hand inside your pocket. This way, it takes some weight off your arm and does not pull on the shoulder. It is almost like wearing a shoulder sling. It helps rest your arm or shoulder and takes some of the weight of the whole arm from pulling down on the shoulder. And yes, you may want to do this for about a day or two until your shoulder feels better.

Another tip for the shoulder to prevent injury (likely repetitive injury) is to avoid reaching forwards for things while crossing your shoulders (reaching across). It is best to move your whole body closer or reach straight forward. This will keep the shoulders from overstretching.

I would suggest researching your condition or injury online and learning about the basic anatomy of your shoulder or whatever body part concerns you. And there are a few simple strengthening and stretching exercises you can also find online to help prevent injury. To give just a couple of simple exercises, you can do is, using the so-called Thera-band or resistance bands. These bands come in different colors, with each color corresponding to certain strength or resistance. Use it by holding it with both hands and pulling it to the side to stretch it. And you can adjust how much resistance and how far you want to move your arms. This movement works certain muscles. The next one is to tie the band to a door or something sturdy in the house and pull it inwards or another direction, so you are using a different muscle group this time. If you are seeing a therapist, they will show you all these other exercises for the shoulder. Remember to do it gently if you are doing it the first time and gradually increase or adjust the resistance and the amount or position of the shoulders or shoulder you are working on. Try to find articles online from a website more suited for you. Something easy for you to understand. You will know right away when the article is not for you. It will be too much information and difficult to read, as it is most likely intended for medical professionals such as physical therapists or orthopedists.

One last thing I want to add here in the shoulder to prevent injury is while you are trying to reposition yourself at night and trying to pull or fix your blanket. This is especially in wintertime when you have this thick and heavy blanket; you want to make sure to move or pull the blanket slowly. Ensure you don't pull it too quickly and forcefully because you are more likely to overstretch your shoulder joint. This movement seemed to over-rotate your shoulders inwards or outwards, and with just enough force, as you pull that heavy blanket, you are more likely to hurt your shoulder this way. This is why it is essential to move slowly, so you will feel your joints when they hurt or are overstretched. I think for most people, as we age, the shoulder joint tends to be weaker than other parts of our body. It is more vulnerable to injury.

Chapter 5

Low Back Hack

Have you ever experienced when you are trying to sleep, and your low back feels uncomfortable? Or can't seem to get comfortable in bed? You want to put something that supports both your legs or knees. Well, how about a pillow under your knees, a small but not too bulky one. Or, you can do a rolled towel also. You can adjust your pillow or towel just under the knees or slightly lower towards your legs. With knees slightly bent or flexed (in medical terms), this trick or hack will take the pull, tension, or pressure on your lower back. Pain or discomfort in your low back may not go right away; you may want to give it time, maybe about 5-10 minutes, as your muscles may need time also to relax.

You can tell if it is helping because the pain will either decrease or increase. But for the most part, you will feel relief from the pain in your lower back. Of course, if you have a severe history of injury to your back that the doctor instructed you not to be in this position, then this is not for you. If you really had acute back pain or when you just hurt your back the day before or that same day, this might only work for a little while, maybe about 15-20 minutes or so (or perhaps even less). You might need to change your position, as that's just how it is when you have acute back pain or pull your lower back muscles that day or the day before. Yes, when it's acute like that, you might need to take some anti-inflammatory medicine (if you can) to help you get comfortable enough to sleep at night.

And while putting this pillow under your legs or knees, watch or move slowly as you want to simultaneously avoid quick movement or twisting on your low back. And yes, if you have a bad back, you may want to keep this in mind, as quick movement and twisting with your low back is a bad thing to do, especially if you have a bad or weak back. Another position for the back is lying on your side with a pillow between your legs to support your top leg to maintain both thighs parallel-like and not crossing. The reason is almost the same as when lying down on your back. It takes the pressure on your low back and keeps your hips and knees in good alignment. You can put the pillow right between the knees or lower towards the legs. So if you have a bad hip or knee, this position is also suitable for hips and knees as it keeps them in a neutral or resting position.

Another position is the prone position or laying on your stomach. Few people can lay on their stomachs as most of us tend to have a belly as we age. But for those who like to lay on their stomach, one tip is to put a pillow (preferably a thin pillow or a rolled towel) under the legs so the knees are slightly bent or flexed. And yes, it's the same reason: to take pressure on your lower back as muscles on the back of the legs (hamstrings) tend to get tight and create tension on the lower back as we age.

Another tip for low back pain is when you are trying to get in and out of bed. We use this trick, or rather I should say, this is the proper way to get in and out of bed. We always taught this when I was working as a physical therapist, especially in the hospital setting, to patients who had just had surgery especially low back surgery. This technique puts less strain on your back and abdominal muscles, which are very painful for patients who have just had abdominal surgery. So the proper way to do it is by trying to roll on your side first. With the top arm, you bring it across your chest to push on the bed while using the elbow or lower arm to push you up to a sitting position at the side of the bed while lowering your lower legs simultaneously. Then when you are trying to get back to bed, you reverse the whole steps. Sitting at the edge of the bed first, then lower your side using that elbow on that side, then bring your lower legs next to the bed, so you are in a side-lying position. Then you roll so you will be lying on your back. And, of course, you do all these movements slowly. You might still feel some pain or spasms at a certain point during these movements, especially when you have acute low back pain or are in a critical or early phase, just like when you just hurt your back that same day or a day or two after you hurt your back. Usually, when you pull a muscle or overstretched ligaments on your spine because of some new or strenuous activity, you will feel it the next day or that morning after you get up. Just like the other body parts, getting better will usually take at least a day or two.

And, of course, while you do these turning or changing positions during the night, you want to keep in mind to do it slowly, so you don't twist or pull any muscles. Yes, you know the saying, "age gracefully"? I think this is what they mean by that. It is about trying to be more aware of how you move and how you move around your surroundings as well. I think it will save us from unnecessary tripping while we walk around and save our bodies from extreme or unnecessary aches and pains.

Chapter 6

The Hip Hack

Have you ever felt uncomfortable in your hip while trying to sleep or during sleeping? Have you ever felt like your hip can't get comfortable and felt the need to stretch or reposition your hip? The hip joint has these muscles called external rotators and internal rotators. As the name itself, it rotates the hip externally or outwards and rotates the hip internally or inwards. Sometimes these external rotators tend to tighten up because of certain positions or things we do in a way that these external rotators work so hard that, like the rest of our muscles in the body, they get sore or tight. And, of course, just like any muscle in the body, it needs rest and eventually to be stretched. So one thing you can do while lying down is to try to lay on your stomach with your legs straight down (no pillow under the leg, this time).

Of course, you do this if you can tolerate laying on your stomach. And yes, you want to keep your upper body (neck, arms, and upper back) as comfortable as possible so your lower body can relax. I usually put my hands together under my forehead or above my head. Or I bring my arms straight down to the sides of my body, with palms facing up. Then I try to feel, ensuring I'm relaxed from the shoulders and down the legs. I relaxed those hip rotator (external rotator) muscles in this case. I would feel my hips slowly rotate towards the bed (or inwards), feeling comfortable and relieved on both hips. This way, the hip area can relax, and this position tends to rotate the hips inwards, giving a little stretch to the external rotator muscles. You will feel the relaxation almost instantly once you are relaxed. So you can stay in this position as long as you are comfortable.

Another position for the hips is when you are lying on your back, which is what I call a frog position. You rest or spread your legs to the sides with a pillow on the sides or under your knees, or you can do one leg with a pillow on the side, slightly under your knee. Ensure the pillow supports your thigh or knee to prevent over-abducting or spreading too far, as the hip can only go so much in that position. You will feel that relief of the muscles in your hip (external or internal rotators) relax.

Another tip is when you lay on your back, you can put a pillow on the side of your thighs so it's supported so that the hips and knees are slightly bent and the hips are not rotated outwards. You want the hips to rest on the pillow to relax.

And when you want to lay on your side, the pillow again between the legs will help maintain the resting position. Lowering the pillow slightly towards the legs, so the hip is rotated slightly inwards will give the external rotators a little stretch.

You can try these different positions and see which works best for you. And as always, you want to move slowly as you change your position and move the pillow around.

There are a couple of things that you can do, like a bit of exercise or stretching, that can also help. This one is only for people who can get on their hands and knees on the floor and have no problem getting up from the floor. Just in case you do try this and have trouble getting up, the trick is to crawl up to a nearby stable chair using your arms to pull and then push you up while simultaneously bending one knee at a time to get on your feet. So the exercise is this: on your hand and knees, rock or move your whole body back and forth gently or slowly. You can adjust the position of your knees so they are at least shoulder-width apart or a little wider. This way, you will feel the stretch in different parts of your hip muscles. This exercise helps stretch the hip and lower back muscles as well. You can do it just a few times, and you can do it as slowly or gently as you can. Then you can slowly go even backward while moving your hands closer, so you almost want to sit on your feet. This will give you a good stretch on the lower back and the back of the hips (buttocks). So while doing all these movements on the floor, you want to keep in mind to move slowly and feel each joint so you don't hurt yourself. Of course, if you had hip surgery or replacement and are unsure if you can do this, check with your orthopedic doctor before trying this movement or exercise.

Also, if you had knee surgery or replacement and are unsure if you can do this movement or exercise, check with your orthopedic doctor first. Also, as we age, our joints get stiff, and they can only bend or rotate so much, just like the knee; in this exercise, you want to be aware and be careful about how your knees respond to this position. As I said, it's always good to move slowly and be mindful of how our body or joints move. You will learn how to listen to your body, and it will tell you that the movement is too much by feeling the pain or stiffness.

Chapter 7

The Ankle or Leg Hack

Have you ever felt an uncomfortable feeling on your leg? Can't get comfortable trying to sleep at night? Like the other body parts, you might have done some activity you are not used to and might have over fatigue certain muscles on your leg or ankle. One example is maybe you did some walking or hiking on uneven ground. Well, this trick or stretch on your leg might help it. It is done best when you try to sit at the side of the bed and cross your leg, so your ankle is on top of your knee. Then try to grab your foot at the bottom by the little toe or the side and pull it towards you slowly. You will feel the stretch on the side of your leg.

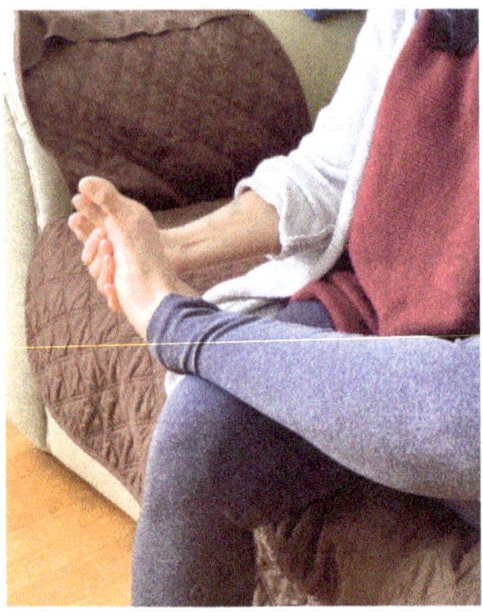

To stretch muscles of the lower leg.

It is also helpful to try to stretch your hamstring muscles (the muscles at the back of your thighs) as, most likely, if your lower legs bother you after a particular activity that you are not used to, these muscles are affected too. Of course, don't forget to do it gently and slowly, as you don't want to do more strain on the muscles. So actually, in this position of stretching your foot or lower leg, if you try to bend your hip or upper body a little forward, like leaning forward, you will feel that hamstring stretch and the muscles on the side of your hip. If you cannot cross your legs or have hip surgery such as hip replacement, I would not advise you to do this unless you know for sure that you can do this movement. So you want to give a gentle stretch and hold it for a few seconds or as you can tolerate and relax, and then you can do it again a couple of times. Of course, you would want to consult your doctor when you have significant swelling and pain in your leg or ankle. Knowing when you need to see a doctor or not is essential. Generally, you would want to see a doctor if you have severe pain, or swelling, on your leg, making sure you don't have anything like a clot on your leg. I am talking about little aches and pains on the body caused by muscle tightness or minor injuries to the muscles that can be annoying, especially when you are trying to sleep at night or even during the day trying to do your regular activities. As for the lower leg or ankle, it is always best to do some gentle stretching, especially before and after a long walk or hiking, to help prevent even minor muscle injuries. Even better, overall body stretching helps prevent injuries.

Chapter 8

Conclusion

I hope these simple hacks or tricks I shared with you will help and hopefully even prevent a severe or annoying injury to your body. Also, avoid an unnecessary visit to your doctor or physical therapist. And also prevent you from taking extra anti-inflammatory drugs that can mess up your stomach or gut. Some people could have prevented some of their injuries from worsening if they had learned to listen to their bodies by being a little patient and being aware of how their bodies move— knowing that the body also needs time to rest or heal. Also, as an advocate for achieving a healthy body, I want to mention the importance of good quality sleep and nutrition. And also, learn more about your condition by researching online.

I believe it is beneficial when you understand your condition well. Of course, you also want to discuss it with your medical doctor for any concerns that may be very important to you. As for me, I also prefer online information that is simple to understand. A few websites that I think are good are WebMD.com, healthline.com, clevelandclinic.org, and nih.org. But there are others and even on Youtube also. But I prefer something simple, not too much information or too long of a video to listen to or read. And the main thing to remember is to move slowly so you can feel or listen to how your body moves; this way, you can prevent injury to your body.